EXTREME!

Pirate!

From Navigation to Amputation

Anna Claybourne

A & C Black • London

Produced for A & C Black by

 MONKEY PUZZLE MEDIA LTD Monkey Puzzle Media Ltd
Little Manor Farm, Brundish,
Woodbridge, Suffolk IP13 8BL, UK

Published by A & C Black Publishers Limited
36 Soho Square, London W1D 3QY

First published 2009

ISBN 978-1-4081-1473-5 (hardback)
ISBN 978-1-4081-1989-1 (paperback)

A CIP catalogue record for this book is available
from the British Library.

Editor: Susie Brooks
Design: Mayer Media Ltd
Picture research: Lynda Lines
Series consultants: Jane Turner and James de Winter

This book is produced using paper that is made
from wood grown in managed, sustainable forests.
It is natural, renewable and recyclable. The logging
and manufacturing processes conform to the
environmental regulations of the country of origin.

Printed in Singapore by Tien Wah Press (Pte.) Ltd

Picture acknowledgements
Alamy pp. 24 (Marion Kaplan), 25 (North Wind
Picture Archives); Art Archive pp. 4–5 (Bibliothèque
des Arts Décoratifs, Paris), 7 (Private Collection), 11
(Private Collection), 22 (Royal Palace, Monte Carlo,
Monaco/Gianni Dagli Orti); Bridgeman Art Library
pp. 13 (Private Collection/Look and Learn), 29
(Private Collection/Look and Learn); Corbis pp. 6
(Bettmann), 9 (Richard T Nowitz), 16 (Tria Giovan),
17 (The Mariners' Museum), 19 (Bettmann), 21
(Bettmann), 26 (Bettmann), 28 (Richard T Nowitz);
Getty Images pp. 1 (Howard Pyle), 18 (Jean Leon
Jerome Ferris), 27 (Howard Pyle); iStockphoto p. 14;
MPM Images pp. 4, 8, 15; National Maritime
Museum, London pp. 10, 12; Science and Society
Picture Library p. 20; Science Photo Library p. 23
(John Burbidge).

The front cover shows a skull and crossed
cutlasses, which often appeared on pirate flags
(MPM Images/Tim Mayer).

CONTENTS

Pirates ahoy!

Look out! PIRAAAATES!!!
A few hundred years ago, everyone feared pirates. These ocean raiders roamed the seas, chasing ships, capturing crews and stealing **cargo**. If you didn't do as they ordered, you might be gruesomely murdered or forced to walk the plank.

Yes, pirates were seriously scary. But they weren't just a bunch of brainless bullies. They had to find their way across vast oceans, keeping their ships afloat and their weapons working. They had to find food and water, cure diseases and treat injuries.

In fact, pirates needed a lot of skills and insider knowledge — from reading the stars to **amputating** limbs.

"Calico Jack" Rackham was a famous pirate known for his stylish dress sense.

cargo goods carried by ship   **amputate** to chop off

The golden age

There have always been pirates, and they still exist today. But most of the pirates in this book lived in the 17th and 18th centuries – the "golden age" of **piracy**.

To capture a ship, pirates sailed up close to it and leapt on board, weapons at the ready.

Axes were handy for chopping through ropes and cabins, as well as attacking victims.

Cutlass

Pirates

Spear

piracy robbery at sea

Sailing the seas

To attack other ships, pirates needed a ship of their own. Small, narrow, speedy vessels were best for chasing and catching their victims.

Pirates loved capturing big, wide ships called galleons, carrying treasure or other valuable loads. These were slow to get moving, and once they were moving, they were hard to stop or turn around.

A small, light ship, such as a ketch or a barque, could move and turn much faster. In one of these, pirates could easily speed up to a bigger ship and **manoeuvre** into a good position to board it.

Scary flags

Pirates really did fly frightening flags, to show other ships that they meant business. Often this was enough to scare their victims into surrendering.

Here's a selection of real pirate flags.

vessel a boat or ship   **manoeuvre** to make a skillful movement

"Jolly Roger" pirate flag

Small size and narrow shape made turning corners easy.

Boat was powered by the **force** of wind in the sails.

Gunports with cannons

This is a model of the Black Falcon, the ship of 17th-century pirate William Kidd.

force a push or a pull

Which way, Cap'n?

How did pirates find their way? In the days before handy **Sat Nav** systems, they had to use the Earth's **magnetism** and their knowledge of the stars.

North Star

These constellations are known as Ursa Major (Great Bear) and Ursa Minor (Little Bear). Ursa Minor contains the North Star, which indicates north.

A compass was essential pirate kit. It's a magnetic needle balanced on a point. The Earth's magnetic pull makes the needle swing around and point north. Once you know where north is, you can also work out south, east and west.

Seafarers also used the positions of the stars and **constellations** to work out their direction and their **latitude** – how far north or south they were.

Astrolabe, used to measure the position of the Sun or a star

Compass

Calipers, used to measure distances on maps

Star patterns

The stars in a constellation can be huge distances apart. But seen from Earth, they seem to form a meaningful shape or pattern.

This old map shows the Atlantic Ocean, the Caribbean and part of North and South America. This region was where many famous pirates hunted their prey.

constellation a group of stars **latitude** distance north or south of the Equator

Tools and technology

Pirate gadgets from 400 years ago might seem old-fashioned to you. But in their day, many pirates were technology lovers who snapped up the latest inventions as soon as they could.

This ship's telescope dates from 1810.

Swinging the lead

Pirates used a lead weight on a string to measure the depth of the sea. This was such as easy job that "swinging the lead" now means messing around and skiving!

The telescope, invented in 1608, used curved glass **lenses** to magnify faraway objects. It helped pirates to spot their victims — and their enemies — before being spotted themselves.

In 1595, John Davis invented the backstaff, which used the Sun's shadow to measure the angle between the Sun and the **horizon**. In the 1730s, the sextant was invented to do the same job for the stars at night. These instruments were used with maps and charts to help pirates work out where they were, when all they could see was sea.

lens a shaped piece of glass used to bend light

A sextant used mirrors to make the Sun or a star appear to line up with the horizon.

1 Look into here.

2 This part is half mirror and half glass window.

3 Move this part around until the star reflected in the mirror lines up with the horizon seen through the window.

4 Read the angle of the star here.

horizon the line where the edge of the Earth seems to meet the sky

Cutlasses and cannons

A good pirate prided himself on his sharp cutlass or well-oiled flintlock pistol. Over the years, pirates' weapons developed and improved to suit the task of capturing enemy ships.

The cutlass was a classic pirate weapon – a small, sharp sword that could be used one-handed, leaving the other hand free. Its short length made it easy to use on a crowded deck.

Blades were often made of steel, a very strong metal made of iron combined with a chemical called **carbon**.

Battle ballistics

Ballistics is the science of firing things like cannonballs. To shoot accurately, pirates had to set the cannon at the right angle, and take into account the wind speed, the speed of the ship and the speed the cannonball would fly at. Tricky!

This curved French cutlass and its **scabbard** were used in the 1790s.

carbon a chemical found in coal, diamonds and living things

1 A "powder monkey" pushed gunpowder into the cannon.

2 Cannonball went in next.

3 Taper was lit to fire the cannon.

4 Holding the "cascabel" (the back end of the cannon) helped to aim it.

It took a team of people to load and fire a cannon.

scabbard a protective case for a sword or dagger

Pieces of eight!

So why did pirates sail the seas, risking disaster and disease? To get rich, of course! The most precious prize of all was treasure, such as jewellery and gold coins.

Silver, gold and gemstones are precious because they are rare. Gold stays valuable for a very long time because it doesn't **react** with other substances — so it won't rot or **rust** away.

Parrots in pirate cartoons say "pieces of eight!" — and these really did exist. They were Spanish silver coins. Doubloons were even more valuable gold coins.

Pirates craved gold and silver coins like these Spanish ones.

Buried treasure

One pirate, William Thompson, is said to have buried a huge treasure hoard on the island of Cocos in the Pacific Ocean, in around 1820. No one has ever found it – yet!

react to change chemically when in contact with another substance

Some treasure was worth fighting for. Clever pirates buried it — or more likely spent it — fast!

Pirates were said to hide their treasure on deserted beaches or islands.

It's mine!

Coins or jewels were kept safe inside a heavy chest.

Iron locks could get very rusty, thanks to oxygen in the air and seawater.

rust a non-reversible change that happens when iron objects react with oxygen and water

Grub and grog

There were no fridges, no freezers and no tin cans. But pirates needed a store of food that would last for weeks at sea.

To stop their food going off, pirates **preserved** it. They dried meat and beans, as removing water from food makes it hard for **germs** to survive. Food could also be salted (like bacon), or pickled in vinegar, as these things kill germs too.

Pirates really did guzzle rum, as well as beer. Alcohol kills germs, so these drinks were safer than plain old water, where germs could breed and grow.

*Pirates ate dried biscuits called hardtack. They were usually crawling with **weevils**!*

Fresh every day

Pirates went fishing too, and stopped at islands to hunt animals and pick fruit. Some kept chickens on board for their eggs, known as "cacklefruit".

preserve to treat food to make it long-lasting   **germs** very tiny living things that cause disease

Pirates often had feasts when they stopped on dry land.

Probably a mixture of rum and water, known as grog

Sluuurp!

What's in here? It could be turtle soup, or salmagundi – a meat, fish and bean stew.

weevil a type of beetle

Bottles of rum or beer

17

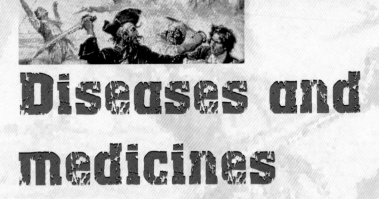

Diseases and medicines

Pirates were far more likely to die from a disease than in a battle. They suffered from tropical diseases like malaria, as well as sunstroke, seasickness, animal bites and stings, and worse.

Most ships had a doctor or **surgeon**, and a medicine chest full of medicines and tools. They used herbal remedies, such as tree bark for malaria, cloves for toothache, peppermint for vomiting, and chamomile for headaches.

Doctors also treated illnesses by cutting the patient to let some blood spurt out. Did it work? Unfortunately for pirates, it didn't.

Blackbeard (left) was one of the most famous of all pirates. He once demanded a medicine chest in return for prisoners he was holding.

surgeon a doctor who carries out operations

18

Pirate James Lind and a fellow seaman prepare a lime to cure scurvy.

Scary scurvy

Pirates often got scurvy, caused by a lack of **vitamin C** from fresh fruit and vegetables. Their skin went pale, their muscles ached and their teeth fell out.

Groan!

Scurvy makes you weak and tired.

Fruits like limes contain plenty of vitamin C – the perfect scurvy medicine.

vitamin a substance essential to the body and found in food

Losing a limb

Pirates really did lose eyes, arms and legs in battle, just like in stories. Limbs were also amputated if they were injured or infected.

Even hundreds of years ago, there were artificial limbs to replace missing arms and legs. Properly shaped ones were expensive, though. On a pirate ship, you'd have to make do with whatever was lying around. So pirates sometimes had a wooden peg-leg, or a metal hook for a hand.

This artificial hand dates from the late 16th century. Silver Arm's silver arm probably looked similar.

Silver Arm

Oruc Reis was a Turkish pirate who lost his left arm in a battle in 1512. He was nicknamed "Silver Arm" after the shiny silver replacement hand he wore.

infected diseased by germs or rotting away

In those days, there was no **anaesthetic**, so having a limb cut off hurt — a lot!

anaesthetic a powerful painkiller

Pesky parasites

A pirate ship was an enclosed, tight space, with lots of men all crammed together. It was heaven for fleas, lice, nits and bedbugs!

In fact, a typical pirate was sure to be home to a variety of biting, nibbling **parasites**. Fleas, nits and bedbugs sucked his blood, while mites fed on his skin flakes. Body lice crawled around in the seams of smelly old pirate pants and shirts.

Ships had their own hangers-on, too. Most were full of rats, while small sea creatures called barnacles collected on the **hull** and slowed the ship down.

These sailors are tipping their ship over to clean barnacles off it – a job known as careening.

Worm damage

Many a pirate ship fell apart thanks to shipworms. They aren't actually worms, but a kind of **clam**. They burrow into underwater wood and fill it with tiny holes.

parasite a creature that lives on or in another living thing

BOINNGG!

This photo shows a human flea at about 50 times life size.

Eggs inside the flea — for making lots more fleas!

Mouthparts for sucking blood.

Powerful back legs allow fleas to leap from one person to another.

hull the main outer body of a ship   **clam** a type of shellfish

What's that smell?

If you could step inside a 17th-century pirate ship right now, there's one thing you'd notice straight away. It would stink!

Pirates ships didn't have showers, and modern toilets hadn't been invented. Pirates could wash in the sea, but they rarely bothered. Most pirates didn't clean their teeth either, so they usually had tooth decay and smelly breath.

For a toilet, pirates used the "head" – a hole in a seat sticking out over the sea at the front of the ship. Waves splashing over the ship's **bow** washed away the mess.

Can you imagine sitting on one of these open-air ship toilets?

Sweaty and stinky

Why does not washing make you whiff? It's mainly sweat collecting on the skin. If it's not washed away, **bacteria** feed on it – and they give off smelly chemicals.

bow the front end of a ship   **bacteria** a kind of germ

Blackbeard demonstrates the many ways in which a pirate could seriously pong.

Bad breath from drinking rum, smoking tobacco and avoiding a toothbrush

Blackbeard wore smoking **tapers** in his hair, which didn't help.

Grimy hair and beard

Sweaty armpits

Phhheww!

Dirty clothes

Unwashed feet

taper a thin candle or paper strip

Sharks and sea monsters

Wild animals were a big part of life for many pirates. They caught them, ate them, and were sometimes eaten by them!

Did pirates really have parrots on their shoulders? It's not clear, but they did capture tropical animals such as parrots and monkeys to sell. European leaders liked keeping **exotic** pets, and paid a high price for them.

Sharks followed ships to eat the scraps — or sometimes dead bodies — thrown overboard. When pirates made their victims walk the plank, the sharks would be waiting.

The sea monster in this illustration looks like a giant octopus (though real ones aren't quite this big).

Sea monsters

Seafarers' stories of sea monsters were thought to be fairytales. But scientists have discovered several huge sea creatures, such as the colossal squid, that could have explained these sightings.

exotic from somewhere far away and unfamiliar

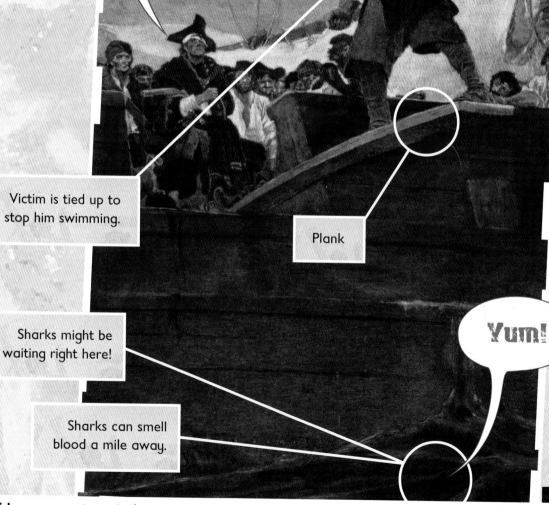

It wasn't common, but pirates sometimes really did make people walk off a plank into the sea.

Victim is tied up to stop him swimming.

Plank

Sharks might be waiting right here!

Sharks can smell blood a mile away.

squid a sea creature similar to an octopus

Davy Jones' Locker

Davy Jones' Locker was what pirates called the bottom of the sea. It was where you were headed if you died at sea, walked the plank, or went down in a sinking ship.

When a pirate died, the body couldn't be stored on board. It had to be buried at sea. Soon, only the skeleton would remain, as the rest was munched by sea **scavengers** such as sharks, shrimps and worms.

When a ship sank to the bottom, it gradually became coated in seaweed and coral. But any treasure on board could stay shiny for hundreds of years, waiting to be found.

Archaeologists bring up gold and silver coins recovered from the Whydah.

The wreck of the Whydah

In 1717, pirate Sam Bellamy captured a treasure ship called the *Whydah*, but it then sank. The wreck was located in 1984, and divers rescued piles of treasure from it.

scavenger an animal that eats dead, rotting bodies

A ship sank fast once it had begun to fill with water.

A sinking ship could suck people down with it, so the crew had to get off fast.

Water sloshed to one side, making the ship tip even faster.

Yikes!

The lucky ones might escape in a rescue boat.

archaeologist someone who studies people and objects from the past

Glossary

amputate to chop off

anaesthetic a powerful painkiller

archaeologist someone who studies people and objects from the past

bacteria a kind of germ

bow the front end of a ship

carbon a chemical found in coal, diamonds and living things

cargo goods carried by ship

clam a type of shellfish

constellation a group of stars

exotic from somewhere far away and unfamiliar

force a push or a pull

germs very tiny living things that cause disease

horizon the line where the edge of the Earth seems to meet the sky

hull the main outer body of a ship

infected diseased by germs or rotting away

latitude distance north or south of the Equator

lens a shaped piece of glass used to bend light

magnetism a kind of pulling force

manoeuvre to make a skillful movement

parasite a creature that lives on or in another living thing

piracy robbery at sea

preserve to treat food to make it long-lasting

react to change chemically when in contact with another substance

rust a non-reversible change that happens when iron objects react with oxygen and water

Sat Nav a navigation system that uses space satellites

scabbard a protective case for a sword or dagger

scavenger an animal that eats dead, rotting bodies

squid a sea creature similar to an octopus

surgeon a doctor who carries out operations

taper a thin candle or paper strip

vessel a boat or ship

vitamin a substance essential to the body and found in food

weevil a type of beetle

Further information

Books

The Usborne Official Pirate's Handbook by Sam Taplin (Usborne Publishing, 2006)
A handy guide to help you make your way as a would-be pirate in the days of sailing ships.

Horribly Famous Pirates by Michael Cox (Scholastic, 2007)
Real-life exploits of a selection of famous pirates, with lots of jokes and cartoons.

Eyewitness: Pirate by Richard Platt (Dorling Kindersley, 2007)
Detailed exploration of pirate life, with lots of fascinating photos.

Piratology by Dugald Steer (Templar Publishing, 2006)
Embark on a thrilling fantasy pirate adventure with interactive features, flaps and extras.

Websites

www.nationalgeographic.com/pirates/adventure.html
Take part in an interactive pirate adventure.

www.nationalgeographic.com/whydah/main.html
Meet Captain Sam Bellamy's crew, the pirates who captured the *Whydah*.

http://pirateshold.buccaneersoft.com/pirate_flags.html
See the scary flags that real-life pirates chose to fly on their ships.

http://jersey.uoregon.edu/vlab/Cannon/
Try entering different numbers to make a cannon fire at a target, just as pirates did.

Films

Pirates of the Caribbean: The Curse of the Black Pearl directed by Gore Verbinski (Disney, 2003)
In this action-packed movie, pirate Jack Sparrow helps to save the heroine Elizabeth from evil pirate captain Hector Barbossa and his haunted ship the Black Pearl. Follow more of Jack Sparrow's adventures in the sequels:
Pirates of the Caribbean: Dead Man's Chest (2006) and ***Pirates of the Caribbean: At World's End*** (2007).

Peter Pan directed by P.J. Hogan (Universal, 2003)
A magical boy whisks three children away from their bedroom to a world of adventures, including a showdown with the evil pirate Captain Hook.

Index